Classic M**OVIE**
INSTRUMENTAL SOLOS

— Contents —

Arranged by Bill Galliford, Ethan Neuburg and Tod Edmondson

© 2010 Alfred Music Publishing Co., Inc.
All Rights Reserved. Printed in USA.

ISBN-10: 0-7390-7001-0
ISBN-13: 978-0-7390-7001-7

DING-DONG! THE WITCH IS DEAD

(from *The Wizard of Oz*)

Music by
HAROLD ARLEN

Track 2: Demo
Track 3: Play Along

Ding-Dong! The Witch Is Dead - 2 - 1
35107

Track 4: Demo
Track 5: Play Along

CANTINA BAND
(from *Star Wars Episode IV: A New Hope*)

By
JOHN WILLIAMS

Moderately fast ragtime (♩ = 112)

Cantina Band - 2 - 1
35107

33

41

49

D.S. %al Coda

Coda

CONCERNING HOBBITS

(from *The Lord of the Rings: The Fellowship of the Ring*)

By
HOWARD SHORE

Track 6: Demo
Track 7: Play Along

35107

JAMES BOND THEME

Track 8: Demo
Track 9: Play Along

By
MONTY NORMAN

Moderately bright (♩ = 138)

With a slight swing feeling

(straight eighths)

35107

Track 10: Demo
Track 11: Play Along

GONNA FLY NOW
(Theme from *Rocky*)

By
BILL CONTI, AYN ROBBINS
and CAROL CONNORS

Moderately ♩ = 96

Gonna Fly Now - 2 - 1
35107

RAIDERS MARCH

Track 12: Demo
Track 13: Play Along

By
JOHN WILLIAMS

Raiders March - 2 - 1
35107

Track 14: Demo
Track 15: Play Along

FAMILY PORTRAIT

(from *Harry Potter and the Sorcerer's Stone*)

By
JOHN WILLIAMS

Slowly, with expression ($\quad$ = 80)

* An easier 8th note alternative figure has been provided.

HEDWIG'S THEME
(from *Harry Potter and the Sorcerer's Stone*)

Track 16: Demo
Track 17: Play Along

By
JOHN WILLIAMS

STAR WARS
(Main Theme)

Track 18: Demo
Track 19: Play Along

By
JOHN WILLIAMS

35107

IN DREAMS
(from *The Lord of the Rings: The Fellowship of the Ring*)

Track 20: Demo
Track 21: Play Along

Words and Music by
FRAN WALSH and
HOWARD SHORE

Moderately slow (♩ = 76)

SONG FROM M*A*S*H*

(Suicide Is Painless)

Track 22: Demo
Track 23: Play Along

Words and Music by
MIKE ALTMAN and JOHNNY MANDEL

35107

OVER THE RAINBOW

(from *The Wizard of Oz*)

Music by
HAROLD ARLEN

PARTS OF AN ALTO SAXOPHONE AND FINGERING CHART

• When there are two fingerings given for a note, use the first one unless the alternate fingering is suggested.

• When two enharmonic notes are given together (F♯ and B♭ for example,) they sound the same pitch and are played the same way.

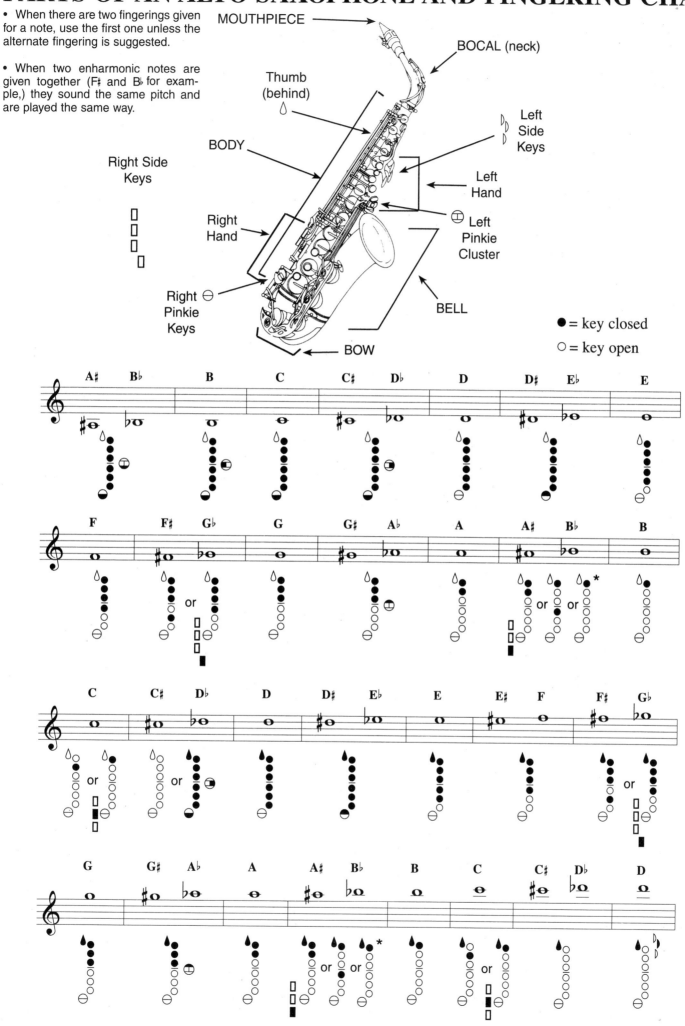

* Both pearl keys are pressed with the Left Hand 1st finger.

KEEP YOUR STUDENTS PLAYING WITH THESE GREAT PLAY-ALONGS

Arranged for Flute, Clarinet, Alto Saxophone, Tenor Saxophone, Trumpet, Horn in F, Trombone, Piano Accompaniments, Violin*, Viola* and Cello*.

* Piano Accompaniment included

LEVEL 1

Easy Christmas Instrumental Solos
Book & CD

Easy Popular Movie Instrumental Solos
Book & CD

Easy Rock Instrumental Solos
Book & CD

LEVEL 2–3

Classic Movie Instrumental Solos
Book & CD

Harry Potter™ Instrumental Solos (Movies 1–5)
Book & CD

Indiana Jones and the Kingdom of the Crystal Skull Instrumental Solos
Book & CD

Lord of the Rings Instrumental Solos
Book & CD

Selections from Rolling Stone Magazine's 500 Greatest Songs of All Time: Instrumental Solos, Volumes 1 and 2
Book & CD

Star Wars® Instrumental Solos (Movies I–VI)
Book & CD

Top Praise and Worship Instrumental Solos
Book & CD

The Wizard of Oz Instrumental Solos
Book & CD

—— Visit **alfred.com** for more information ——

INSTRUMENTAL ENSEMBLES FOR ALL SERIES

Arr. Michael Story

A versatile, fun series intended for like or mixed instruments to perform in any combination of instruments, regardless of skill level. All books are in score format with each line increasing in difficulty from grade 1 to grade 3–4. Perfect for concerts with family and friends, recitals, auditions, and festivals. Available for brass, woodwinds, strings, and percussion.

Movie Duets for All

Titles: Double Trouble • In Dreams • Singin' in the Rain • The Entertainer • Twistin' the Night Away • We're Off to See the Wizard • Be Our Guest • Fame • Wonka's Welcome Song • Wizard Wheezes • Can You Read My Mind? • Star Wars • Everything I Do • I Don't Want to Miss a Thing • Living in America • Gonna Fly Now • Superman Theme.

Movie Trios for All

Titles: Believe • As Time Goes By • Can't Fight the Moonlight • How the West Was Won (Main Title) • If I Only Had a Brain • Nimbus 2000 • You've Got a Friend in Me • Mamma Mia • Batman Theme • Cantina Band • Imperial March • James Bond Theme • Theme from Ice Castles (Through the Eyes of Love) • You're the One That I Want • Raiders March.

Movie Quartets for All

Titles: Hedwig's Theme • Over the Rainbow • And All That Jazz • The Magnificent Seven • Theme from A Summer Place • Eye of the Tiger • There You'll Be • Blues in the Night • The Pink Panther • You're a Mean One, Mr. Grinch • Parade of Charioteers • Hakuna Matata.

Alfred